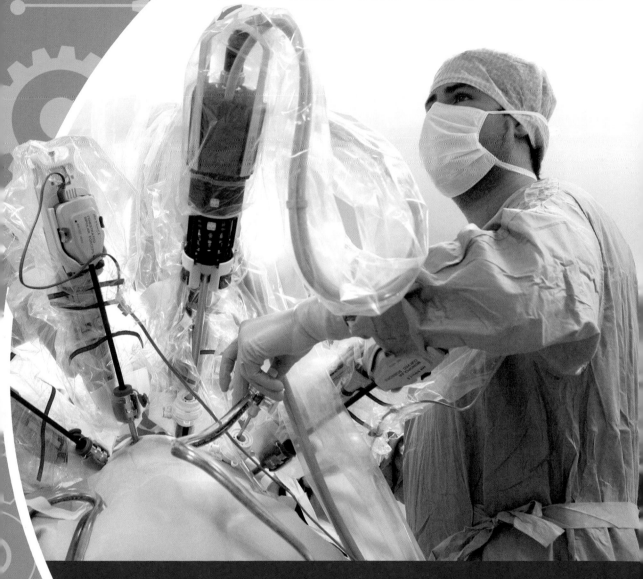

ROBOT
INNOVATIONS

MEDICAL
ROBOTS

BY KATHRYN HULICK

CONTENT CONSULTANT
Michael Yip, Assistant Professor of Electrical
and Computer Engineering
University of California, San Diego

Core Library

Cover image: A surgeon uses the da Vinci Surgical
System to operate.

An Imprint of Abdo Publishing
abdopublishing.com

abdopublishing.com

Published by Abdo Publishing, a division of ABDO, PO Box 398166, Minneapolis, Minnesota 55439. Copyright © 2019 by Abdo Consulting Group, Inc. International copyrights reserved in all countries. No part of this book may be reproduced in any form without written permission from the publisher. Core Library™ is a trademark and logo of Abdo Publishing.

Printed in the United States of America, North Mankato, Minnesota
032018
092018

Cover Photo: Jean-Paul Chassenet/Science Source
Interior Photos: Jean-Paul Chassenet/Science Source, 1; Jacob Ford/Odessa American/AP Images, 4–5; ©[2018] Intuitive Surgical, Inc., 9; Arturo Fernandez/Rockford Register Star/AP Images, 10; Sasin Tipchai/Shutterstock, 12–13; Roger Ressmeyer/Getty Images, 15; Okauchi/Rex Features/AP Images, 18; Christy Radecic/Stryker Orthopaedics/AP Images, 20–21; Rex Features/AP Images, 22; Chinatopix/AP Images, 26–27; Riken/Rex Features/AP Images, 31, 45; Yamaguchi Haruyoshi/Corbis News/Getty Images, 32; Peter Menzel/Science Source, 34–35; Gustoimages/Science Source, 39 (top); Elise Amendola/AP Images, 39 (middle); Jonathan Hayward/The Canadian Press/AP Images, 39 (bottom), 43; Philippe Psaila/Science Source, 40

Editor: Bradley Cole
Imprint Designer: Maggie Villaume
Series Design Direction: Ryan Gale

Library of Congress Control Number: 2017962828

Publisher's Cataloging-in-Publication Data

Names: Hulick, Kathryn, author.
Title: Medical robots / by Kathryn Hulick.
Description: Minneapolis, Minnesota : Abdo Publishing, 2019. | Series: Robot innovations | Includes online resources and index.
Identifiers: ISBN 9781532114687 (lib.bdg.) | ISBN 9781532154515 (ebook)
Subjects: LCSH: Surgical robots--Juvenile literature. | Robotics in medicine--Juvenile literature. | Medicine--Technological innovations--Juvenile literature. | Robots--Juvenile literature.
Classification: DDC 610.28563--dc23

CONTENTS

CHAPTER ONE
Surgery, Robot Style **4**

CHAPTER TWO
Developing Medical Robots **12**

CHAPTER THREE
Robotic Helpers **20**

CHAPTER FOUR
Would You Trust a Robot? **26**

CHAPTER FIVE
From Snakebots to Cyborgs **34**

Fast Facts. 42

Stop and Think. 44

Glossary 46

Online Resources 47

Learn More 47

Index 48

About the Author 48

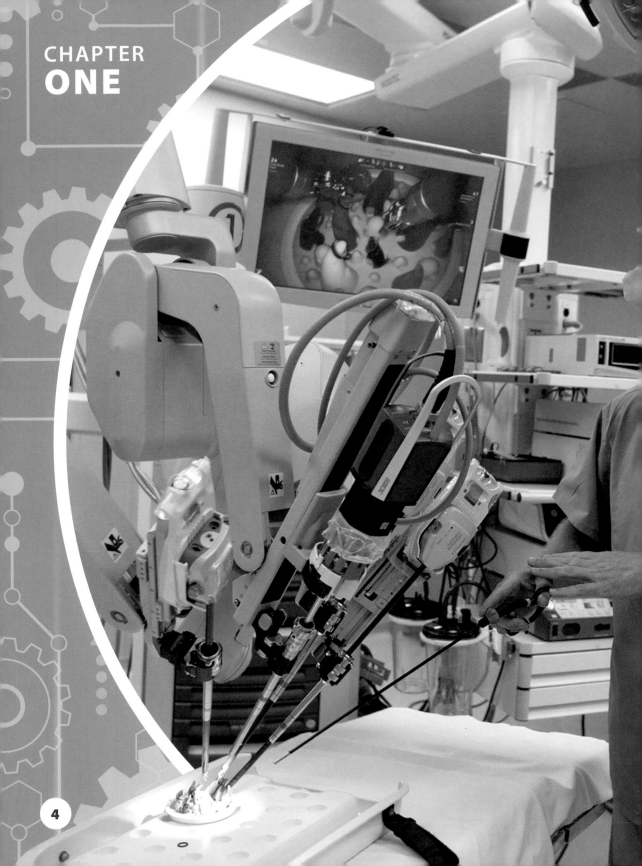

SURGERY, ROBOT STYLE

A human surgeon makes a few tiny cuts in a patient's body. Then she walks away. But the surgery hasn't even started yet. What's going on? The surgeon won't perform this surgery with her own hands and eyes. She'll use a robot. The da Vinci Surgical System has four robotic arms. Each arm lowers into the patient's body. One arm bears a tiny camera. The others hold pincers, graspers, or clippers. The surgeon sits nearby at a console. She grasps hand controllers and positions her feet over pedals.

A surgeon explains how the da Vinci Surgical System is less invasive than other methods.

A HIGH-RISK VIDEO GAME

Performing robotic surgery is a bit like playing a video game. The surgeon watches a screen showing the inside of the body. She moves the controllers to operate robotic tools. The stakes are very high. A successful operation can mean the difference between life and death for a patient.

This patient has cancer. The cancer formed a tumor on one of his kidneys, which are the organs that remove waste from a person's body. The surgeon must take out the entire tumor. This will prevent the cancer from spreading to other areas of the body.

DRIVERLESS SURGERY

The da Vinci robot cannot do anything without a human operator. But surgical robots are beginning to learn how to operate on their own. In 2016, a surgical robot called STAR (Smart Tissue Autonomous Robot) sewed up pig intestines on its own. The robot made better stitches than human surgeons.

Robots help make surgeries easier for the surgeon and safer for the patient. The robot replaces human hands and eyes with high-tech tools. Instead of two hands, the surgeon now has four. These tiny robot hands can make smaller, more precise motions than human fingers. The robot camera can zoom in to help the surgeon see better.

With a special light, the robotic system can even make certain parts of the body glow. First, assistants add a dye into the patient's blood. The dye glows green in this special light. The bloodstream quickly carries the dye into healthy parts of the kidney. But blood flow does not reach the tumor. On screen, the kidney now glows green. The tumor looks dark gray. It's very easy to see where to cut. In the past, a surgeon might have removed the entire kidney. That way, she wouldn't risk leaving some of the tumor behind. Now, this patient can keep his kidney. He likely will go home cancer-free.

DESIGNING ROBOTS

CATHERINE MOHR

Catherine Mohr loves to tinker with machines. She worked as a bicycle mechanic in high school. She got a degree in engineering, then went to medical school. Robots weren't a big part of medicine at the time. That soon changed. Mohr combined her engineering and medical background to work on robotic surgical systems. She is the director of medical research at Intuitive Surgical, maker of the da Vinci Surgical System. The company released the first da Vinci system in 2000. This brought the age of robotic surgery. The company has continued to develop new robotics technology for surgery.

A ROBOT INVASION

The da Vinci Surgical System is just one of many robots that help surgeons in the operating room. Robots help perform operations on many parts of the body. Other areas of health care rely on robots as well. In hospitals, mobile robots deliver meals, medication, and supplies. They also cart trash and dirty laundry away. Cleaning robots help mop floors. Pharmacist robots

MEET THE DA VINCI
ROBOT

The da Vinci has four arms for performing surgeries. How might having four arms be better than two? All four are controlled by one person. How is one person controlling all four arms better than two people controlling two arms each?

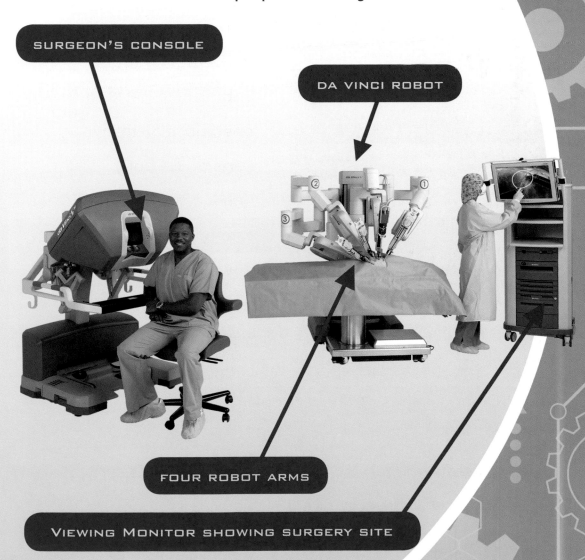

SURGEON'S CONSOLE

DA VINCI ROBOT

FOUR ROBOT ARMS

VIEWING MONITOR SHOWING SURGERY SITE

A woman uses her new robotic arm for simple tasks in her daily life.

act like vending machines to dispense medication. Nursing robots remind patients to take pills. They also answer questions and help people in and out of bed. Some people are even becoming cyborgs. A cyborg is a person with robotic parts. Robotic arms, legs, and exoskeletons allow people with disabilities to perform daily tasks. And tiny machines called nanobots soon might help monitor a person's health from inside the body.

Robots are changing health care. Medical robots take over jobs that are too precise, repetitive, or dangerous for people. They help make health care safer. They also free up human workers to spend more time with patients. Medical robots have the potential to help patients live long, healthy lives.

FROM NEED TO FINISHED PRODUCT

Many people help in making a new robot. For an engineer to design a medical robot, someone must invent the technology first. The ideas for new technology often come from university research. From there, engineers will design robots and program them. Doctors will help guide engineers. But a robot can't help anyone if it isn't used. Hospitals must agree to use brand-new technology. Then doctors can finally use the new medical robot to help patients.

CHAPTER
TWO

DEVELOPING MEDICAL ROBOTS

Robots haven't always been a part of health care. In the 1960s, most robots worked in factories. These robots were generally robotic arms that moved parts and drilled holes. One early robot called Unimate put cars together on assembly lines. Robots quickly became an essential part of any factory.

Some operations aren't that different from what happens in a factory. A surgeon may need to drill a precise hole or hold a body part in place. In the 1980s, some surgeons tried using robots in the operating room. Robots were

Robotic arms help manufacture cars.

DESIGNING ROBOTS

YIK SAN KWOH

Yik San Kwoh was born in China. He came to the United States to study electrical engineering. At Memorial Medical Center in Long Beach, California, he invented new ways to use technology in medical procedures. In 1982, his team started a new project. They planned to use an industrial robot for brain surgery. They developed new tools to make this possible. They practiced on watermelons. They used the robot to find and remove a tiny pellet inside fruit. Finally, Kwoh and his colleagues made medical history. They performed the world's first robotic surgery.

useful even for complex surgeries. Before robots performed surgery, the Arthrobot had already helped in the operating room. Arthrobot held a patient's leg during knee surgery. This job was too boring and tiring for human assistants.

BRAIN SURGERY

The first robotic surgery happened in 1985. Surgeons and engineers at Memorial Medical Center in Long Beach, California,

Dr. Yik San Kwoh poses with the PUMA 200 to demonstrate how the robot aids in biopsy surgery.

operated on a brain tumor. They used a robot arm

called the PUMA 200. It had been made for a factory.

But it was redesigned to help with surgery. The robot

adjusted the drill and held it steady for the surgeon. The surgeon pushed the robot-guided drill into the patient's skull. Then the surgeon inserted a needle held by the robot into the brain. The robot used a brain scan as a guide. It helped make a smaller, more precise hole than a human could. Finally, the surgeons removed a small piece of the tumor for testing.

SHAKEY FINDS A WAY

Any advance in robotics may impact medicine. In the late 1960s, researchers at Stanford Research Institute (SRI) in California created a robot named Shakey. It looked like a washing machine on wheels. But its computer could make a map of its surroundings. A human didn't need to provide directions. This led to mobile robots that drive themselves around. They carry, fetch, and move items in warehouses, hotels, and hospitals.

REMOTE CONTROL

Some research groups have designed robots that allow surgeons or doctors to work from afar. This is called telepresence. The doctor operates the robot like a remote-control car. The National

Aeronautics and Space Administration (NASA) hoped that telepresence would allow doctors on Earth to treat astronauts in space. The United States Defense Advanced Research Projects Agency (DARPA) wanted a robot that could operate on wounded soldiers while in the field.

Robotic systems for surgery in outer space or on battlefields don't exist yet. But these research efforts have led to surgical robot development. The first da Vinci robot came out in 2000. Two years later, surgeons located in New York used the ZEUS robotic system to operate on a woman in France. In most cases, however, the surgeon performing robotic surgery sits in the same room as the patient.

MAKING ROBOTS MORE HUMAN

Some research groups have designed robots that resemble people. These are called humanoid robots. In 2000, ASIMO became the first robot to walk on two legs. ASIMO also could open or close doors and flip

ASIMO greets King Felipe VI and Queen Letizia of Spain in 2017.

light switches. Japanese car and technology company Honda designed the robot to help older people. But ASIMO is still not quite ready for use in the home.

Engineers also craft social robots. These machines attempt to imitate human speech, body language, or even emotions. Social robots often serve as friendly helpers or entertaining toys. But they also help educate children with disabilities. Or they can keep older patients company. Humanoid robots and social robots seem less like machines and more like companions.

FURTHER EVIDENCE

Chapter Two covers important events in the history of medical robots. What ties all of these advances together? Describe the main point of the chapter. Then find three key pieces that support the main point. Next, read the article about the history of the da Vinci Surgical System at the website below. Find a quote from the website that supports the chapter's main point. Does this quote support existing evidence in the chapter, or provide new evidence?

INTUITIVE SURGICAL: HISTORY OF THE DA VINCI SURGICAL SYSTEM
abdocorelibrary.com/medical-robots

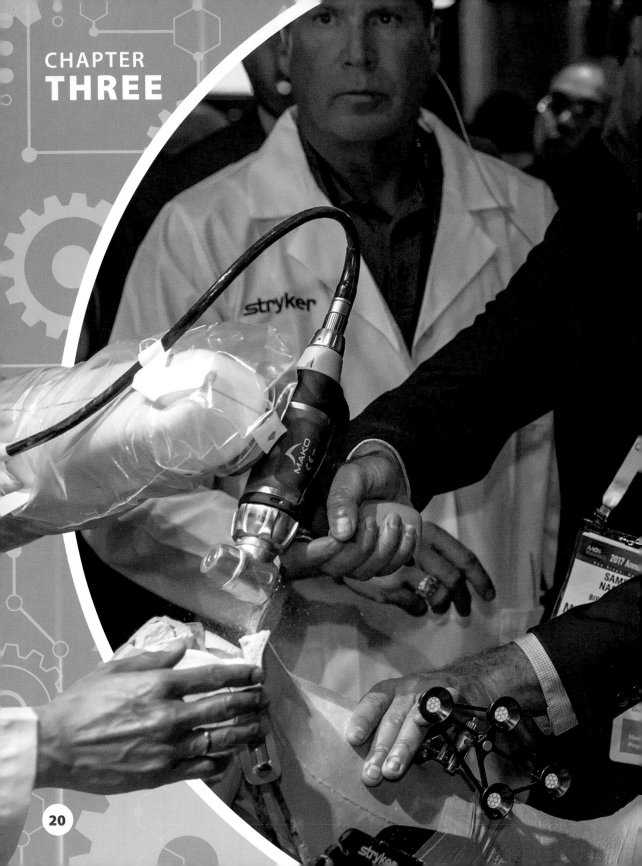

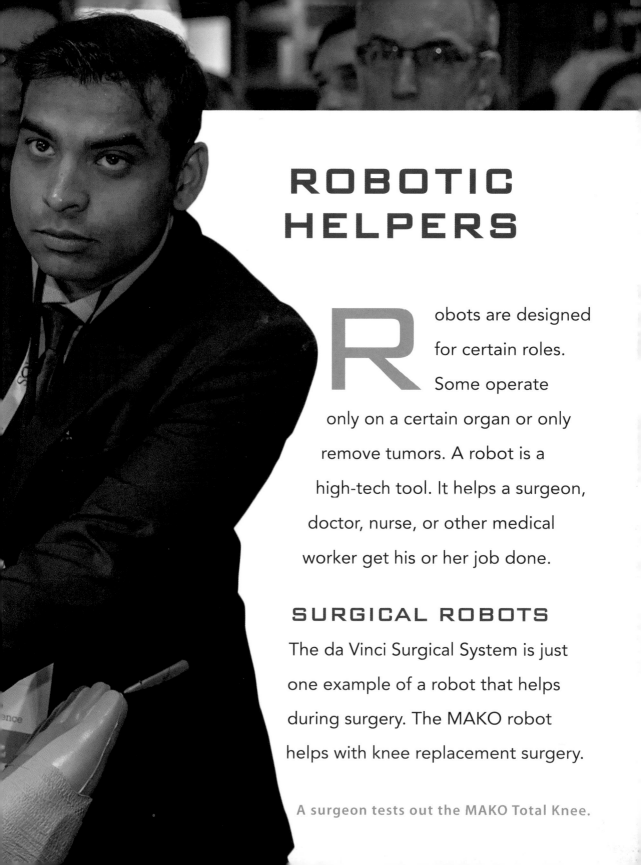

ROBOTIC HELPERS

R obots are designed for certain roles. Some operate only on a certain organ or only remove tumors. A robot is a high-tech tool. It helps a surgeon, doctor, nurse, or other medical worker get his or her job done.

SURGICAL ROBOTS

The da Vinci Surgical System is just one example of a robot that helps during surgery. The MAKO robot helps with knee replacement surgery.

A surgeon tests out the MAKO Total Knee.

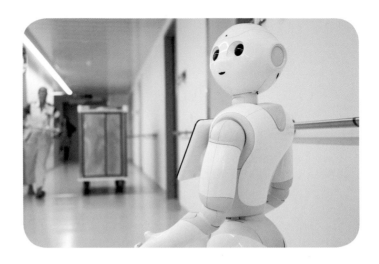

The Pepper robot greets patients in hospitals in Belgium.

This robot uses scans of the patient's bones to plan the procedure. Then it cuts through the bone to make room for a new joint.

CyberKnife is a robot used for cancer treatments. Despite its name, it doesn't cut anything. Instead, it focuses a beam of radiation on a tumor. The Robotic Retinal Dissection Device (R2D2) specializes in eye surgery. The first robotic eye surgery took place in 2016.

HOSPITAL HELPERS

TUG looks like a small cabinet that rolls around on wheels. A fleet of 27 of these robots works at Mission Bay Hospital in San Francisco, California. They bring meals and medication to patients' rooms. This helps the hospital stay organized. It also frees up human workers for more important jobs.

A TUG robot going to the pharmacy to pick up medication might meet another robot there. PillPick is a room-sized pharmacy robot. It is packed with conveyor belts, pipes, and arms that suction up pills.

ROBO-DOCTORS AND NURSES

Telepresence robots allow a doctor to visit patients anywhere. These robots host video calls. The robot RP-VITA drives itself to a patient's room. There, the doctor video-calls the patient

SQUEAKY CLEAN

Robots help keep hospitals clean. A children's hospital in Oahu, Hawaii, dressed up its mopping robots to look like a train and a school bus. Other robots don't need soap and water to clean. They use ultraviolet light instead. Shining this light kills dangerous germs. However, the light also harms people. The UV-Disinfection Robot drives itself into an empty hospital room. Then it goes from place to place, shining light until it hits every area.

DESIGNING ROBOTS

IBM

The computer company IBM designed Watson Health. It is a computer program that diagnoses cancer. Watson Health can sort through huge amounts of medical information faster than humans. So, a doctor can use it to help make faster, more informed decisions. Watson Health has been used as part of an eldercare robot named Multipurpose Eldercare Robot Assistant (MERA). MERA can remind patients about medication or appointments. Watson Health's knowledge grows as it gets new data.

using a screen on the robot's head.

Watson Health is another form of medical robot. It acts as a virtual mind. Watson Health uses artificial intelligence (AI) to diagnose diseases or perform medical research. AI takes in data and uses it to make decisions.

Social robots combine a robot body and mind. Pepper is the size of a child. It has a cute face and a computer screen in its chest. The robot greets and helps guests in two hospitals in

Belgium. Pepper and similar social robots may soon fetch things patients need. Or they may remind patients about appointments and medication.

IMPROVING HUMAN CARE

Even with robots, human workers remain important. Medical robots aren't meant to take over health care from humans. They enhance humans' abilities. They allow surgeons to operate with better vision and greater precision. They allow doctors to visit patients from afar. They perform jobs that are tiring or boring. This frees up people to do more important work.

EXPLORE ONLINE

Read the section of this chapter about the TUG robot. What jobs does the robot do? Why do you think a hospital might choose to use TUG robots? Now visit the website below. Read about ways that TUG can help a hospital. Now answer the same questions again. What new information did you learn?

THE JOBS OF MEDICAL ROBOTS
abdocorelibrary.com/medical-robots

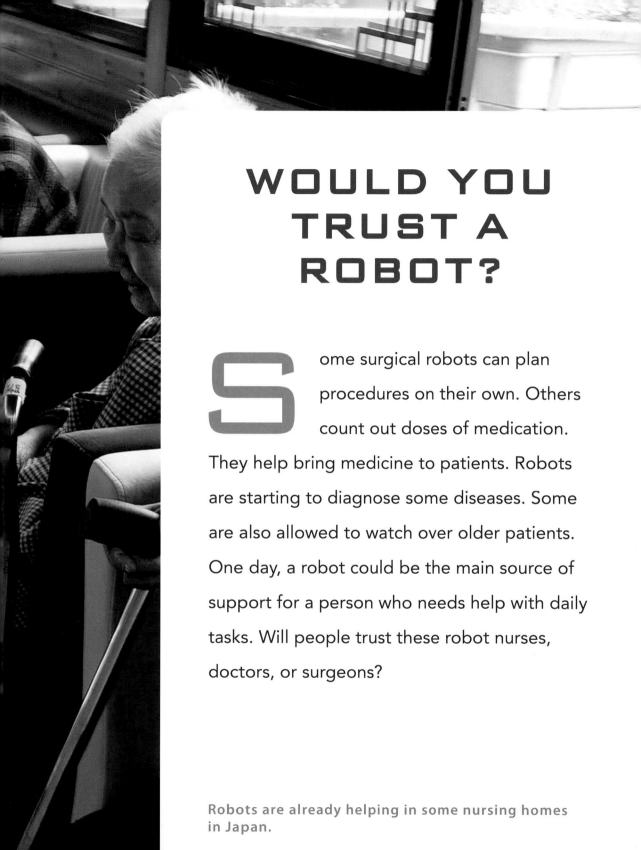

WOULD YOU TRUST A ROBOT?

Some surgical robots can plan procedures on their own. Others count out doses of medication. They help bring medicine to patients. Robots are starting to diagnose some diseases. Some are also allowed to watch over older patients. One day, a robot could be the main source of support for a person who needs help with daily tasks. Will people trust these robot nurses, doctors, or surgeons?

Robots are already helping in some nursing homes in Japan.

DEADLY MISTAKES

Medical robots work very closely with patients. Some people might fear trusting a robot with a medical task. A pharmacist robot could make a deadly mistake by selecting the wrong medication. Or a robot caretaker could fail to notice a patient in distress.

However, robots tend to make mistakes less often than humans when doing certain tasks. They must be extremely safe and dependable, or no one will use them. For example, pharmacy robots make far fewer mistakes counting pills than people do. Also, human doctors and nurses sometimes are tired or stressed. This can lead to errors. Robots' batteries can run down, but they cannot be stressed. They always perform in the same, predictable manner.

KEEPING THE CARE IN HEALTH CARE

Accurate, predictable, safe treatment isn't the only important part of medicine, though. Patients also need emotional support. They want doctors and nurses who listen to their hopes and fears. Some experts worry that robots will take the "caring" out of health care. A machine might perform a procedure perfectly. But if the patient feels afraid or uncomfortable, then the machine didn't do the whole job.

Engineers realize how important it is for patients to trust medical robots. Most robots that work closely with people have cartoonish features. This is supposed to help

DESIGNING ROBOTS

ROBOTS IN ELDERCARE

The amount of older people needing daily care is growing. Some think robots can help with basic tasks. Robots could help people living on their own or in retirement homes. Robert Sparrow, who studies bioethics, argues that robots replacing human workers won't happen soon. Sparrow says there are several ways that robots could help workers, but replacing humans will make problems. Nurses or cleaners often provide most of the social interaction that older people receive.

JUST HUMAN ENOUGH

Pepper is a robot that has human features. Its eyes are wide black dots circled with green or blue light. It has speakers where a person's ears would be. Some other robots look much more lifelike. The Albert Einstein HUBO is a robot with an Albert Einstein head attached. It looks lifelike and mimics facial expressions. Many people think it's creepy. People don't trust robots that look too much like machines. But they also tend not to like robots that look too human. The experience of interacting with a human-like robot feels awkward or even scary. For this reason, most successful social robots, such as Pepper, have cartoonish features.

patients feel relaxed. The Robear, for example, is a robot that lifts patients out of bed and into a wheelchair. Robear has a cartoon bear face. A hospital in San Francisco plans to outfit its TUG delivery robots to look like fruit. A friendly appearance can inspire trust as a robot performs tasks.

Some medical robots are designed for friendship. PARO looks like a baby seal. It responds to petting with happy sounds.

Robear demonstrates lifting a patient out of a hospital bed.

PARO, a seal robot, is used in some nursing homes to provide interaction with older adults.

Several nursing homes have used PARO to help calm and comfort elderly patients. Sadly, there aren't enough human nurses and caretakers to fulfill the world's needs. Robots may be the only answer.

STRAIGHT TO THE
SOURCE

Isaac Asimov was a scientist and science-fiction author who wrote many stories about robots. In his story "Runaround," robots had to follow three basic laws. These laws made an ethics system for robots. Ethics are general rules that help determine right and wrong.

A robot may not injure a human being or, through inaction, allow a human being to come to harm.

A robot must obey orders given it by human beings except where such orders would conflict with the First Law.

A robot must protect its own existence as long as such protection does not conflict with the First or Second Law.

Source: "Do We Need Asimov's Laws?" *MIT Technology Review*. MIT, May 2014. Web. Accessed December 7, 2017.

What's the Big Idea?

Take a minute to think about how these laws work together. What is the most important concept for robots according to these laws? Can you think of a situation in which the rules might not guide correct behavior? Are there any other robot rules that you would add?

FROM SNAKEBOTS TO CYBORGS

The medical robots of the future likely won't be large metal machines. Metal makes sense in a factory. But metal parts can easily hurt human bodies. Soft or flexible robots could provide better safety and comfort. The future may also bring tiny robots that patrol inside people's bodies. And cyborg limbs or robotic clothing will help people with disabilities lead normal lives.

A robot is covered in padding and touch sensors to interact with humans safely.

DESIGNING ROBOTS

RODNEY BROOKS

Rodney Brooks knows robots. At the age of four, he earned the nickname "the professor." At 12, he built an electronic tic-tac-toe game from scratch. Now, his robots work in homes and businesses. He cofounded the company iRobot. It makes the Roomba cleaning robot. Brooks also founded the company that makes the factory robot Baxter. Unlike most factory robots, Baxter safely works side by side with people. One day, Baxter could help older people with daily tasks. Brooks' main concern about the future of robotics is that there won't be enough robots to go around.

SNAKES, OCTOPUSES, AND WORMS

Most of today's robotic surgeries involve cutting into the body. These incisions take time to heal. Some new surgical robots don't need any incisions. They enter the body through the mouth or another opening.

Flexible robots slide through the body like snakes or octopus arms. A camera at the robot's tip shows the way. Once at the surgery site, instruments emerge from inside the robot. The surgeon controls the instruments from a console.

Flexible robots can work outside the body too. Axsis is a new surgical robot still in the design phase. Each of its two tiny arms is about the same width as a spaghetti noodle. These arms can twist and bend. A surgeon controls their motions from a console. Axsis could one day help perform surgery on the eyes.

TINY ROBOTS

To a nanobot, a spaghetti noodle would seem wider than a highway. Nanobots are very tiny robots. They are not visible to the naked eye. One day, these tiny robots may patrol inside people's bodies. They could watch for disease, make repairs, or bring medication. But a future in which nanobots keep us healthy is still far off.

These tiny machines are hard to build. There's no room inside for motors or other parts. And to a tiny robot, blood seems as thick as molasses. Getting a nanobot to move through the body isn't easy.

Some engineers have experimented with using magnets outside the body to guide nanobots.

CYBORGS

Robotic body parts are another big part of health care. People who have lost an arm or leg may get a robotic one as a replacement. A person with paralysis may use a robotic suit to walk. These robots turn a person into a cyborg. Some people with robotic limbs can control them using their thoughts. In 2001, Jesse Sullivan became the first person to do this.

Researchers are adding sensors to

MIND CONTROL

Jesse Sullivan lost both of his arms in an accident. The nerves that controlled the arms still ran up to his brain. The nerves were like wires that no longer connected to anything. Sullivan's doctor connected those arm nerves to muscles in Sullivan's chest. Then he put sensors near those muscles. The sensors control a robotic arm. All Sullivan has to do is think about moving his arm. A muscle in his chest twitches. The twitch moves the robotic arm.

ROBOTS WORK WITH
THE BODY

Believe it or not, these strange-looking devices all have robotic features! They are all designed to work with the human body. How does a robot's design affect its use?

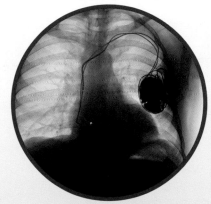

Pacemakers have sensors that monitor whether a heart is beating too slowly or out of rhythm. With Wi-Fi enabled devices, data can be uploaded from the pacemaker to a doctor. If the heart is out of rhythm or stops, the pacemaker can also restart the heart.

This robot is designed to be swallowed. Once in the stomach, it unfolds and performs procedures. The robot is still being tested.

Limbs can be replaced with robotic versions. These new limbs can help the person hold objects or even walk again.

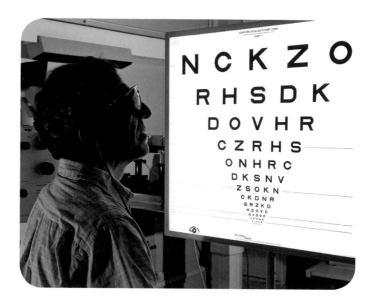

The ARGUS II helps restore functional vision to a patient with blindness

robotic limbs. These sensors will be able to send touch sensations back to the user's brain. Robotic systems can also bring back other missing senses. Robotic implants in the ears can help patients with deafness hear. And the Argus II robotic system can restore some functional sight to patients with blindness. The system sends information from a camera to the brain.

In the future, nursing robots will also become more humanlike thanks to improved intelligence. Medical robots might no longer simply be tools. They could become an essential part of people's lives and health.

STRAIGHT TO THE
SOURCE

Jan Scheuermann went through brain surgery as part of a scientific experiment. The surgeons put implants in her brain. She used those implants to control a robotic arm with her mind. In an interview, she describes making the decision to go through with the surgery:

> *At the time, I had been a quadriplegic for twelve years. I hadn't moved anything. I'm paralyzed from the neck down. I was determined I was going to move that robotic arm. I was reassured that this was an excellent surgeon, so I wasn't worried about safety. The [researchers] did tell me that I'd have two caps coming out of my skull for a year. I barely heard them say it. . . . Whatever I had to do, I was going to do it. . . . I named the implants Lewis and Clark, because they were going to lead an expedition into the brain and look for new pathways and chart new territory.*
>
> Jan Scheuermann, email to author, February 17, 2016.

Back It Up

Jan Scheuermann is using evidence to support her decision. Write a paragraph describing the decision she made. Then write down two or three pieces of evidence she used to back up her decision.

FAST FACTS

- Medical robots assist surgeons, doctors, nurses, and other health-care workers. These machines typically perform tasks that are repetitive, difficult, or dangerous for people.

- The first robotic surgery took place in 1985. Since then, robots have become a normal part of many surgeries. A human surgeon always guides the robot's every move.

- Surgical robots do not move by themselves yet, but many groups are working on this. An autonomous robot could be introduced first for doing tasks that are small, tedious, and need to be done, but do not get in the way of the doctors.

- Some medical robots are becoming more independent. It's very important for these robots to interact safely with people. Patients must feel comfortable around the robots that care for them. A cute appearance can improve trust.

- In hospitals, mobile robots carry meals, medication, and supplies to patient rooms. They cart trash and dirty laundry away. Robots also help keep hospitals clean.

- A telepresence robot is like a virtual body for a doctor or nurse. The robot allows a doctor to video chat with patients anywhere in the world. The doctor can use the robot to assess a patient from afar.

- Nursing robots are designed to help patients with daily tasks. Some robots specialize in helping people get in and out of bed. Or the robot may remind a patient about medication or appointments.

- Some social robots provide therapy to people with disabilities. These robots may also provide entertainment or companionship.

- A cyborg is a person with a robotic body part. Some people with disabilities use robotic arms, legs, or bodysuits. Robotic systems can also help restore missing senses, such as touch, hearing, or sight.

- In the future, soft and flexible medical robots will likely become more common. Tiny robots may work inside the body, performing repairs or delivering medication.

STOP AND
THINK

Say What?

The medical industry uses a lot of technical vocabulary. Learning about robotics involves encountering new terms, too. Find five words in this book you've never heard before. Use a dictionary to find out what they mean. Then write the meanings in your own words, and use each word in a new sentence.

You Are There

Chapter Two discusses early medical robots. Imagine that you were there for the very first robotic surgery. Write 200 words describing what the experience was like. Use facts from the real event, but also describe how you feel while watching the surgery.

Tell the Tale

Chapter Four introduces robots that make deliveries in hospitals. Imagine that you are working alongside a TUG robot in a hospital. What tasks does the robot do? Which tasks can only you do? Tell the story of your day. How do you and the robot help make people's lives easier?

Dig Deeper

After reading this book, what questions do you still have about medical robots? With an adult's help, find a few reliable sources that can help you answer your questions. Write a paragraph about what you learned.

GLOSSARY

cyborg
a person or animal with mechanical body parts

ethics
the study of right and wrong behavior

humanoid
resembling a person

nanobot
a microscopic robotic machine

nerve
a wirelike fiber that carries signals between the brain and parts of the body

pharmacist
a person who prepares and gives out medication

quadriplegic
someone who has paralysis in both arms and legs

radiation
waves of energy that can be used to kill cancer cells

sensor
a device that collects information from the world

surgeon
a doctor who performs procedures that involve cutting or manipulating the body

telepresence
the ability to be virtually present at a distant event using technology

tumor
an abnormal growth in the body

ONLINE RESOURCES

To learn more about medical robots, visit our free resource websites below.

Core Library
CONNECTION
FREE! COMMON CORE MULTIMEDIA RESOURCES

Visit **abdocorelibrary.com** for free Common Core resources for teachers and students, including vetted activities, multimedia, and booklinks, for deeper subject comprehension.

Booklinks
NONFICTION NETWORK
FREE! ONLINE NONFICTION RESOURCES

Visit **abdobooklinks.com** for free additional online weblinks for further learning. These links are routinely monitored and updated to provide the most current information available.

LEARN MORE

Schulman, Mark. *TIME For Kids Explorers: Robots*. New York: TIME for Kids, 2014.

Swanson, Jennifer. *Everything Robotics*. Washington, DC: National Geographic Kids, 2016.

INDEX

artificial intelligence, 24

ASIMO, 17, 18,

Axsis, 37

console, 5, 37

CyberKnife, 22

cyborg, 10, 35, 38

DARPA, 17

da Vinci Surgical System, 5, 8, 9, 17, 19, 21

humanoid, 17, 19

MAKO, 22

nanobot, 10, 37–38

PARO, 30, 32

Pepper, 24, 30

PillPick, 23

PUMA 200, 15

Robear, 30

robotic arm, 5, 10, 13, 38, 41

robotic limb, 38–40

Robotic Retinal Dissection Device (R2D2), 22

RP-VITA, 23

sensors, 38, 39, 40

Sullivan, Jesse, 38

surgeons, 5–7, 8, 9, 13, 14–16, 17, 21, 25, 27, 37, 41

telepresence, 16–17, 23

TUG, 22, 23, 25, 30

tumors, 6–7, 15–16, 21–22

Watson Health, 24

ZEUS robotic system, 17

About the Author

Kathryn Hulick is a freelance writer and former Peace Corps volunteer. She has written many books and articles for children. She lives in Massachusetts with her husband, son, dog, and a Roomba robot.